—Food—
GARNISHES
A N D
DECORATIONS

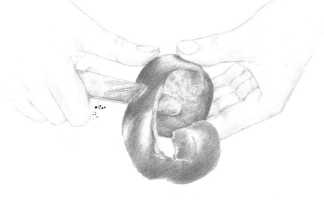

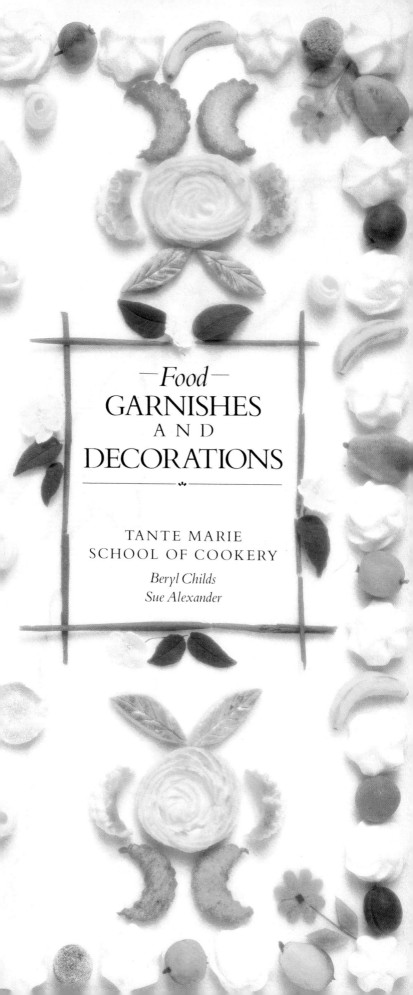

—Food—
GARNISHES
A N D
DECORATIONS

TANTE MARIE
SCHOOL OF COOKERY

Beryl Childs
Sue Alexander

CONTENTS

First published in 1984 by
Octopus Books Limited
59 Grosvenor Street, London W1

Third impression, 1986

© 1984 Hennerwood Publications Limited

ISBN 0 86273 136 4

Printed in Hong Kong

INTRODUCTION

This book contains a variety of our ideas on the presentation of food. As you become familiar with the garnishes and decorations shown here, you will be able to enjoy adapting them, even to invent more of your own.

The word garnish refers to savoury foods whilst decoration is applied to sweet. With either you should choose something that will both contrast with and complement the colours and texture of the food. It is a mistake to disguise the food completely and the garnish/decoration should have some link with the ingredients used in the food itself. For instance, a garnish of whole prawns complements a prawn vol-au-vent, whilst whole turned mushrooms would work well on a mushroom quiche, besides which both these garnishes will also suggest to the guest what type of filling is inside. When you can, keep the temperature of the food and its garnish/decoration alike – a cold vegetable garnish on hot food is not very appetizing.

As well as choosing the appropriate garnish/decoration take care with the arrangement of food itself on the plate. A fairly plain or lightly patterned plate is best and a variety of differently shaped plates will make food look attractive for a buffet or larger dinner party. Place a garnish/decoration away from the very edge of the plate, otherwise it becomes difficult to carry without touching the food. If the recipe is served with a sauce (or syrup), coat the food first and only allow the sauce to flow over the plate if you intend covering the whole plate; a partly covered plate looks messy. Keep a herb, vegetable or fruit garnish/decoration clean and fresh-looking by not letting it sink into the sauce (or syrup) and by having it ready to place on the food at the last moment. Whole sprigs of parsley are particularly difficult to remove from a sauce and not especially nice to eat.

In this book we have purposely kept the use of specialized equipment to a minimum. With just a few good sharp knives of various sizes and a few basic ingredients you can instantly enjoy making many of the garnishes/decorations before experimenting with any other equipment.

To help you decide which foods to use each garnish and decoration with we have given some suitable suggestions in brackets below the instructions.

Where a garnish or decoration can be made in advance, we have also included the following symbols with any useful information on storage alongside:

□ may be made the day before
● may be made up to 3 days beforehand
★ may be frozen

—THE—
ART OF
CUTTING

❧

For a neat result it is always important to use sharp knives for cutting — and it is also much safer than exerting excessive pressure on a blunt knife. Try also to keep your cut garnishes and decorations to a similar size.

Dull, limp or stale-looking fruit or vegetables look unappetizing so buy the best quality produce. Marks and blemishes all tend to show.

Julienne vegetables

1 Use celeriac, turnip, potato or carrot and start by cutting the vegetable into a neat block.

2 Cut into even slices about 3 mm/⅛ inch wide.

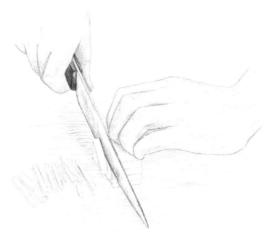

3 Stack the slices into a neat block, slice into 3 mm/⅛ inch julienne strips.

4 Blanch for 1 minute, refresh under cold water and drain.

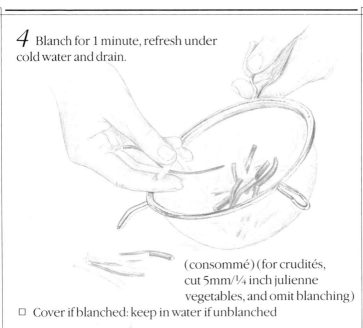

(consommé) (for crudités, cut 5mm/¼ inch julienne vegetables, and omit blanching)

☐ Cover if blanched: keep in water if unblanched

Julienne fruits

1 Peel the rind from orange, lemon, grapefruit or lime removing all pith. Straighten the edges and cut into julienne strips.

2 Blanch for 1 minute and refresh under cold water. (caramelized oranges, poached pears) ☐ Keep in water

Tomato rose

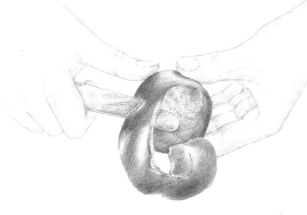

1 Use a firm tomato and with a sharp knife remove the skin in a continuous strip about 1 cm/½ inch wide, starting at the smooth end.

2 With the flesh side inside, start to curl from the base end, forming a bud shape between the fingers.

3 Continue winding the strip of skin into a rose.

(salads, cold meats)

Tomato water-lily

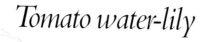

1 Hold the tomato between the thumb and forefingers and with a small sharp knife make zig zag cuts around the middle.

2 Carefully separate the two halves and place a small sprig of parsley in the centre of each.

(salads, cold meats)

Olive flower

Using black or green olives and a sharp paring knife slice petal shapes from the unstoned olive. Arrange the petal shapes to form a large or small flower as required.

(grated carrot salad, hard-boiled eggs, pâté)

Radish rose and radish water-lily

1 For a radish rose, remove the stalk and with the pointed end of a small sharp knife cut a row of petal shapes round the radish keeping them joined at the base.

2 Cut a second row of petal shapes in-between and above the first row and continue cutting rows of petals until the top of the radish is reached.

1 For a radish water-lily, remove the stalk and using a small sharp knife cut through 4-6 times, keeping the radish joined at the base.

Place both radish rose and water-lily in iced water for several hours to open out.
(cheeseboard, salads)   □ Keep in water

Celery curls and spring onion tassels

1 For celery curls, cut the celery into even lengths and cut down each end several times and in each direction, keeping the celery joined in the middle. As an alternative, cut the celery curls in half and stand them upright to serve.

1 For spring onion tassels, remove the root from the spring onions and trim to about 7.5 cm/3 inches. Cut lengthwise through the stalk several times to within 4 cm/1½ inches of the end.

Place both curls and tassels in iced water for about 1 hour to open out.
(cheeseboard, dips and oriental-style dishes)   □ Keep in water

Lemon, orange and cucumber slices

1 Holding a canelle knife firmly use the notch to remove strips of skin at regular intervals down the cucumber.

2 Cut into even slices.

1 Prepare orange or lemon in the same way, removing any pips when slicing.
(trout, drinks) ☐ Lemon only: keep covered

Cucumber and lemon cones

1 Thinly slice cucumber and/or lemon and cut from centre to edge.

2 Hold each side and twist to form a cone.

1 Alternatively, hold a slice of cucumber and lemon together and twist as in step 2 to make an attractive cone.
(salmon steaks, smoked salmon) □ Lemon only: keep covered

Cucumber, lemon and orange peel spirals

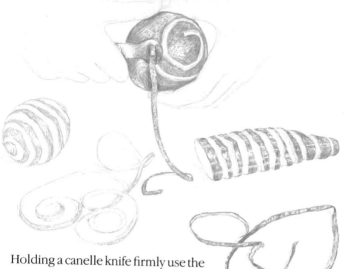

Holding a canelle knife firmly use the notch to remove a strip of skin or peel.
Continue to remove the skin or peel in a spiral fashion from the vegetable or fruit. Arrange attractively over the side of a glass or over a dessert.
(cucumber, lemon and orange spirals for drinks) (lemon and orange spirals for poached pears) □ Wind round in a tight spiral and secure

Gherkin fan

1 Using a sharp knife slice through the gherkin at regular intervals, keeping it joined at the base.

2 Gently pull out the slices to form a fan.
(cheeseboard, hors d'oeuvre)
• Keep covered

Carrot rolls

1 Clean a large carrot and using a potato peeler remove strips.

2 Roll each strip to make a curl and secure with a cocktail stick. Place in iced water for about 1 hour to keep their shape.

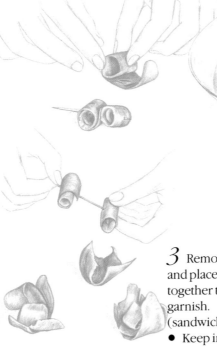

3 Remove the cocktail stick and place 2 or 3 curls together to form an attractive garnish.
(sandwiches, cheeseboard)
• Keep in water

Spring onion and pepper lily

1 Cut a petal shape slice from the side of a red pepper and prepare a straight spring onion by removing the outer layer and root.

2 Make an incision in the pepper petal 'and push the spring onion through. Arrange one or more at the side of a platter.
(hors d'oeuvre, cold meats, buffet foods)

Lemon and cucumber butterflies

1 Cut thin slices from a lemon or cucumber and cut each slice in half. Keeping the lemon or cucumber joined in the middle cut through the outer edge towards the centre.

2 Open out to form a butterfly.
(salmon, smoked salmon, prawn cocktail)
□ Lemon only: keep covered

Turned mushrooms

Choose even-sized button mushrooms. Using the point of a small sharp knife score the cap from the centre to the edge removing a small amount of flesh each time. Cook in the usual way. (steaks, crown roast, fish dishes)

Turned carrots, turnips and celeriac

1 Peel the vegetable and cut into even-sized pieces.

2 Hold the piece of vegetable between thumb and forefinger and cut into barrel shapes tapering the vegetable at the top and the base and turning the vegetable as you go. Cook in the usual way and toss in butter.
(poultry, meat) □ Keep uncooked vegetables in water

Bouquetière

Prepare a selection of Turned vegetables (see left). Arrange them alternately with the addition of cooked peas, French beans, onions, etc., glazed in butter.
(crown roast, lamb noisettes)

Orange and grapefruit flower

1 Cut a slice from the top and bottom of one orange and grapefruit with a serrated knife.

2 Stand the fruit on one of the cut ends and cut away the skin and pith until all the flesh is exposed.

3 Hold the fruit at the top and bottom and cut between the membrane to remove each segment, folding back each membrane as you go.

4 Arrange orange and grapefruit segments alternately into a flower.
(florida cocktail, duck, fruit salad)   □   Keep segments of each fruit separate and covered

Orange, lemon and tomato baskets

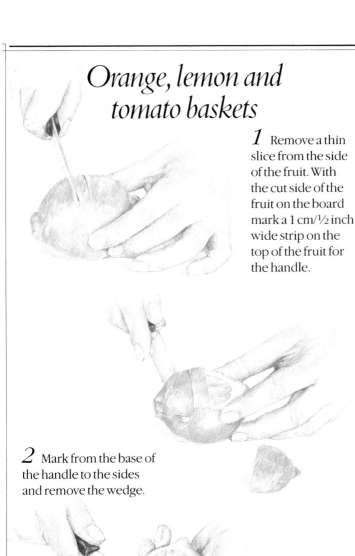

1 Remove a thin slice from the side of the fruit. With the cut side of the fruit on the board mark a 1 cm/½ inch wide strip on the top of the fruit for the handle.

2 Mark from the base of the handle to the sides and remove the wedge.

3 With a grapefruit knife or serrated spoon scoop out the flesh from under the handle, and inside the basket.

4 Fill as required with watercress, or mustard and cress. (buffet table) ☐ Orange and lemon only: keep covered

Kiwi, melon and pineapple baskets

1 Remove a thin slice of skin from the base of the fruit.

2 Using a small sharp knife cut out a lid by making zig zag cuts just below the top of the fruit.

3 Carefully remove the lid. Scoop out the flesh, leaving the base intact, and, if necessary, chop roughly. If using a melon discard the seeds. Mix the flesh with a suitable liqueur, and with other fruits, and put back into the basket.

4 Replace the lid at a slight angle, allowing the fruits to show at one side. (fruit salads)

Polonaise

1 Finely chop some fresh parsley.
Chop the white of a hard-boiled egg.

2 Sieve the yolk of a
hard-boiled egg.

3 Fry some
breadcrumbs in
butter.

4 Sprinkle in
layers over a
vegetable.
(cauliflower,
cabbage,
Brussels sprouts)
□ Keep
ingredients
separate, ready
to be assembled

Viennoise

1 Prepare the ingredients as for Polonaise (see left) steps 1-3 and have ready several lemon slices (p. 15) cut in half.

2 Cut another thin lemon slice and sprinkle a neat ring of parsley in the middle. Place a halved anchovy curl in the centre.

3 On the outside of a serving dish arrange the slices of lemon in a ring adding the chopped egg white then the chopped parsley followed by the sieved yolk of egg. Place the slice of lemon with the anchovy curl on the centre of the food. (veal escalopes, pork escalopes, steaks)   □ Keep ingredients separate, ready to be asembled

Lemon pig

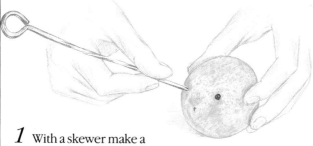

1 With a skewer make a
hole on either side of the
pointed end of a lemon and fill each hole with a black pepper-
corn to form the eyes.

2 With a sharp knife cut a flap on either side of the lemon to
make the ears.

3 Insert short pieces of cocktail sticks for the legs and a piece
of parsley stalk for the tail.
(hors d'oeuvre, buffet table)   □ Uncovered or covered

Anchovy lattice

1 Soak the anchovies in
milk for about 15 minutes
to remove excess salt. Dry
well on paper towels.

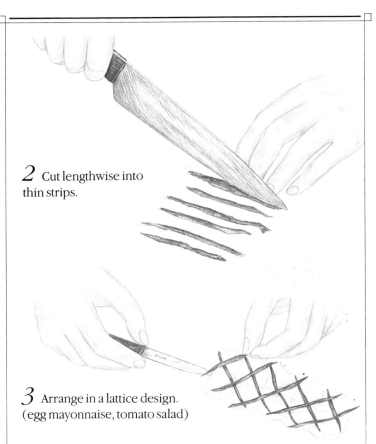

2 Cut lengthwise into thin strips.

3 Arrange in a lattice design. (egg mayonnaise, tomato salad)

Below: Egg mayonnaise, as part of mixed hors d'oeuvre; garnished with anchovy lattice (left)

Cutlet frills

1 For a cutlet or poultry frill, use a piece of plain white paper about 25 cm/10 inches long and cut a strip 9 cm/3½ inches wide.

2 Fold lengthwise to within 1 cm/½ inch of the top of the paper.

3 Make a series of thin cuts 3.2 cm/1¼ inches in from the folded edge along the length of the paper.

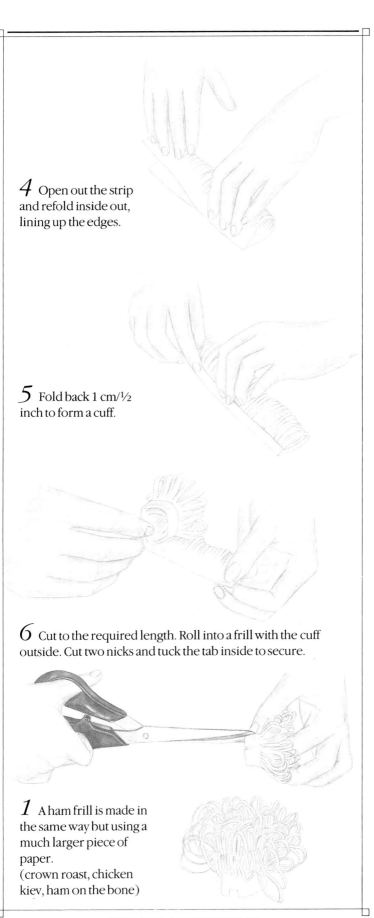

4 Open out the strip and refold inside out, lining up the edges.

5 Fold back 1 cm/½ inch to form a cuff.

6 Cut to the required length. Roll into a frill with the cuff outside. Cut two nicks and tuck the tab inside to secure.

1 A ham frill is made in the same way but using a much larger piece of paper.
(crown roast, chicken kiev, ham on the bone)

—POTATO,—
CURLS AND
CROÛTONS

❧

*Choose a variety of potato which
will suit the form of garnish and start with
evenly sized potatoes. Any leftover potato
pieces can be used to make creamed
potatoes or added to home-made soups.*

*For butter balls and curls you
should use butter straight from the
refrigerator. For croûtons it is best to use
bread which is one day old, and a good
safeguard against uneven slicing is to buy a
cut loaf!*

Game chips

1 Peel the potatoes and slice evenly and very thinly using a sharp knife or a mandolin (taking care to keep fingers well away from the blade).

2 Soak in cold water for 10 minutes to remove the starch. Drain and dry thoroughly on paper towels.

3 Fry in hot fat in a chip pan or deep fryer for 3 minutes or until golden brown. Drain well and sprinkle with salt. (roast chicken, roast pheasant, dips)
□ Keep uncooked chips in water

Pommes de terre noisette

1 Peel large potatoes and press a parisienne cutter/melon baller right into the potato until a half circle is made. Scoop out small balls.

2 Blanch for 2 minutes then drain and dry thoroughly on paper towels.

3 Fry in hot butter in a shallow pan for 5-7 minutes shaking from time to time until golden brown and tender. Drain well. (steaks, lamb cutlets) □ Keep uncooked noisettes in water

Gaufrettes

1 Peel the potatoes and using a mandolin with a corrugated cutter remove 1 slice from the potato and discard (taking care to keep fingers well away from the blade).

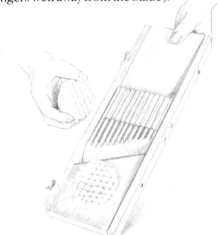

2 Give the potato a ¼ turn and slice again. You may have to adjust the thickness of the blade to give a criss cross pattern. Continue in this way, giving a ¼ turn between each slice.

3 Soak in cold water for 10 minutes to remove the starch. Drain and dry thoroughly on paper towels.

4 Fry in hot deep fat in a chip pan or deep fryer for about 4 minutes or until golden brown. Drain well and sprinkle with salt. (dips, grilled meat, fish) □ Keep uncooked gaufrettes in water

Potato baskets

1 To make a basket, line a mesh draining spoon, or 1 small metal sieve, with uncooked sliced Gaufrettes (see left) or Game chips (p. 34). Place another mesh draining spoon or small metal sieve on top and fry in hot deep fat in a chip pan or deep fryer until golden brown.

2 Remove the spoons or sieves and sprinkle the potato basket with salt. (fill with peas or watercress or leave empty) □ Keep in sealed container

Paille

1 Peel potatoes and cut into very fine Julienne strips (p. 8). Rinse and dry thoroughly on paper towels.

2 Fry in hot deep fat in a chip pan or deep fryer until golden brown. Drain well and sprinkle with salt.

(mixed grills, snacks)   □ Keep uncooked paille in water

POMMES DE TERRE DUCHESSE
Put 750 g/1½ lb boiled potatoes through a metal sieve or vegetable mill into a warmed basin. Beat in 25 g/1 oz butter, 2 egg yolks, salt and freshly ground black pepper, and continue beating until a creamy consistency is obtained.

CHOUX PASTRY
Put 150 ml/¼ pint water and 25 g/1 oz butter in a saucepan and heat gently until the butter has melted. Bring to the boil and immediately add 50 g/2 oz of sifted plain flour. Beat well until thickened to a smooth glossy paste which leaves the sides of the pan. It may be necessary to keep the saucepan over the heat for a moment or two. Beat in 1 egg yolk then gradually add 1 beaten whole egg until the mixture becomes smooth, thick and shiny.

Pommes de terre duchesse border and nests

Fill a nylon piping bag containing a large rosette nozzle with Pommes de terre duchesse mixture (see left).

1 For a border, butter the edge of the serving dish and pipe a design round it.

1 For a nest, grease a baking sheet. Pipe a ring starting in the centre and working outwards to about 6 cm/2½ inches in diameter, then continue piping on top of the outer ring.

2 For both border and nests brush lightly with beaten egg and brown in the top of a preheated hot oven (220°C, 425°F, Gas Mark 7) for about 10 minutes.
(border for lamb, poached fish) (fill nests with cooked peas or mixed vegetables) ☐ Keep uncooked border and nests uncovered in refrigerator ★ Keep uncooked border and nests, and cook from frozen for about 25 minutes

POMMES DE TERRE DAUPHINE
Mix together 1 quantity of Pommes de terre duchesse and 1 quantity of Choux pastry (p. 38).

Potato lengths and crowns

Note: If the potato mixture disintegrates during frying it is too soft. This can be corrected by beating in a little extra flour.

1 For lengths, place the Pommes de terre dauphine mixture (see above) in a piping bag containing a 1 cm/½ inch plain nozzle. Pipe 2 cm/1 inch lengths into hot deep fat in a chip pan or deep fryer, cutting them off with a sharp knife. When golden brown remove and drain well.
(sweetbreads, brains, liver)

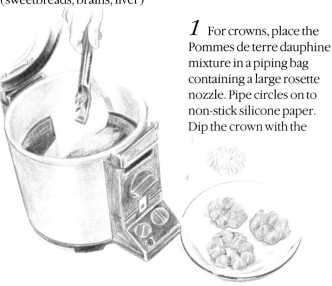

1 For crowns, place the Pommes de terre dauphine mixture in a piping bag containing a large rosette nozzle. Pipe circles on to non-stick silicone paper. Dip the crown with the

paper (holding the sheet of paper uppermost) into hot deep fat in a chip pan or deep fryer and the crowns will slide off. Cook for 8-10 minutes.
(fill crowns with cooked peas or mixed vegetables)

Butter curls and butter balls

1 For butter curls, using a block of cold butter and a butter curler dipped in hot water draw the curler across the surface.

1 For butter balls, using a block of cold butter press a parisienne cutter melon or butter baller right into the block and scoop out butter balls.

Drop each curl or ball into iced water to keep its shape. (cheeseboard and with dinner rolls) ☐ Keep covered in iced water

Plain croûtons

1 Use a 1 cm/½ inch thick slice of day-old bread, remove the crusts and cut into even dice.

2 Heat equal quantities of butter and oil and when very hot fry the dice until golden brown. Alternatively deep fry in oil. Drain immediately on paper towels.   (soups)   □ Uncovered

Garlic-flavoured croûtons

Make as for Plain croûtons (see above) but fry 1 large peeled

garlic clove for about 3 minutes and remove before adding the bread. Do not deep fry flavoured croûtons.   (soups)

Left: Watercress soup; garnished with shaped croûtons (below) and swirl of cream.
Assorted savoury mixtures; served in bread tartlets (below) with fresh fennel, parsley
and thyme

Shaped croûtons

Cut the shape with canapé or aspic cutters. Fry as for Plain
croûtons (p. 43) and drain immediately on paper towels.
(larger croûtons round veal and poultry casseroles or as a base
for canapés) (smaller croûtons for soups) □ Uncovered

Bread tartlet

1 Use a 5 mm/¼ inch slice of fresh bread and cut a circle
about 7.5 cm/3 inches in diameter. Dip in melted butter and
use to line a tartlet tin.

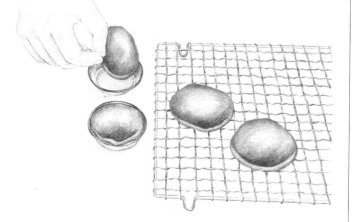

2 Bake in a preheated moderate oven (190°C/375°F/Gas Mark
5) for 15 minutes or until golden brown. Cool on a wire tray.
(fill with savoury mixtures for starters)

CLEAR-CUT
ASPIC

You will find that bought aspic powder is a quick and easy substitute for making aspic yourself, simply follow the packet's instructions for making up the powder. It is well worth working out your design on a flat surface before transferring it on to the food. Afterwards, spoon over a final coating of liquid aspic.

Diced jellied stock

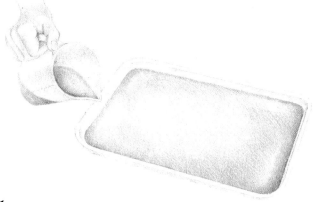

1 Use 600 ml/1 pint of aspic jelly strengthened with 10 g/¼ oz (2 heaped teaspoons) of gelatine, dissolved. Pour into a shallow tray and leave in the refrigerator to set.

2 When set loosen the edges by gently breaking the seal with the fingertips and turn out on to dampened greaseproof paper.

3 Cut into neat cubes.
(round a turned out terrine, raised pie, chaudfroid dishes)
☐ Keep covered in the refrigerator

Decorations for aspic work

☐ With all aspic work keep completed dishes in the refrigerator overnight

Chevron

1 Dip a sprig of tarragon in boiling water then refresh with cold water and dry well.

2 Dip 1 leaf at a time in liquid aspic and arrange in a chevron design.
(whole salmon, trout)

Lily of the valley

1 Cut small circles from hard-boiled egg white using a plain piping nozzle and remove 1 or 2 tiny wedges from one side of the circle with the point of a sharp knife.

2 Cut a thin strip of blanched tarragon, chive or julienne strip of cucumber (see Chevron) and dip in liquid aspic. Arrange on the food to form a stalk. Dip each circle of egg white in liquid aspic and carefully arrange along the stalk with the cut edge turned outwards.
(salmon or ham mousse)

Geometrical design

1 Blanch strips of orange or lemon rind, carrot, red or green pepper for 1 minute. Cut tiny diamonds either with an aspic cutter or a small sharp knife and work out an arrangement with the edges touching to form a larger diamond shape.

2 Dip in liquid aspic and transfer the design to the food. (chaudfroid chicken joints or turkey, mousses)

Flower design

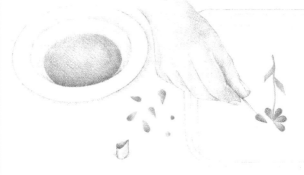

1 Blanch strips of red or green pepper, carrot, orange or lemon rind for 1 minute. With an aspic cutter or a small sharp knife remove petal shapes from the vegetable or fruit. Work out a flower design with a small circle of lemon rind or red pepper in the centre and using a strip of blanched tarragon, cucumber skin or chive (see Chevron p. 49) to make leaves and a stem.

2 Dip in liquid aspic and transfer the design to the food.

(chaudfroid chicken joints or turkey, salmon)

Bumble bee

1 Slice a piece lengthwise from a black olive and a similar piece from hard-boiled egg white (or lemon rind blanched for 1 minute) keeping both pieces the same thickness.

2 Slice both pieces into equal size strips and arrange alternately to form the body.

3 Cut a circle of olive using a small plain piping nozzle to form the head.

4 Cut a tiny piece of hard-boiled egg white or blanched lemon rind and place on the head to represent the eye.

5 Cut 3 strips of olive for the legs and 2 strips of olive or blanched lemon rind for feelers, and place these in position.

6 Use a tear-drop shaped aspic cutter to make 2 wings from blanched lemon rind and place in position.

7 Having worked out the arrangement, dip one piece at a time in liquid aspic and transfer the design to the food. (chaudfroid chicken joints, mousses)

As a variation this alternative bumble bee needs 2 eyes, 6 legs, and 4 wings.

Inverted moulds

1 Line 1 large mould or several dariole moulds with a thin layer of aspic jelly and leave until firm.

2 Place a dipped decoration (from the selection on the preceding pages) and/or a herb leaf on to the jelly. Allow to set.

3 Cover with another thin layer of aspic jelly and allow to set.

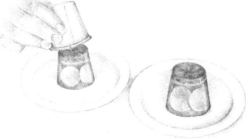

4 Fill the mould as required, e.g. with small slices of cooked vegetables, ham or prawns and top up with liquid aspic, or fill with a mousse mixture.
□ Keep in the refrigerator

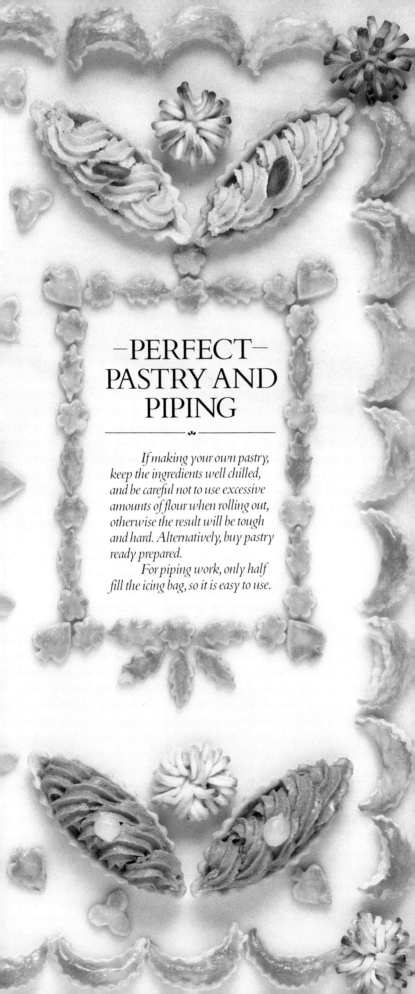

–PERFECT–
PASTRY AND
PIPING

❖

*If making your own pastry,
keep the ingredients well chilled,
and be careful not to use excessive
amounts of flour when rolling out,
otherwise the result will be tough
and hard. Alternatively, buy pastry
ready prepared.*

*For piping work, only half
fill the icing bag, so it is easy to use.*

Edgings for open tarts

A   Cut 1 cm/½ inch circles from a strip of pastry and place in position, brushing the pastry with water.

B   Make 2.5 cm/1 inch cuts around the edge. Brush the pastry edge with water and fold corners down to form triangles.

C   Make 2.5 cm/1 inch cuts around the edge. Brush the pastry edge with water and fold back alternately.

(savoury or sweet tarts)   ● or ★ depending upon filling

Crimping pastry edges

Press the thumb or forefinger of one hand on to the rim and use the thumb and forefinger of the other hand to make crimps.

(tarts or pies)   ● or ★ depending upon filling

Knocking up and fluting

1   Hold the pastry with a floured finger and knock up by tapping the edges of the pastry with the back of a knife.

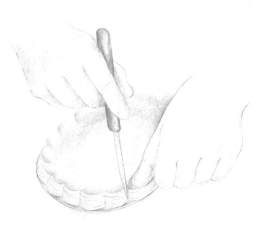

2 Hold the pastry lightly with the thumb and draw the back of a knife across the knocked up edge.
(savoury or sweet pies)   ● or ★ depending upon filling

Pastry tassel

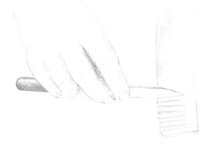

1 Cut a strip of pastry 4 cm/1½ inches wide. Make a series of thin cuts 2.5 cm/1 inch deep.

2 Carefully roll the strip of pastry and stand it up allowing the tassel to open out. Brush the pastry with water to attach the tassel to a pie.
(raised pies, steak and kidney pie)   ● or ★ depending upon filling

Pastry leaves

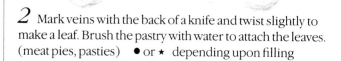

1 Cut a strip of pastry
about 2.5 cm/1 inch
wide and make
diamond shapes.

2 Mark veins with the back of a knife and twist slightly to
make a leaf. Brush the pastry with water to attach the leaves.
(meat pies, pasties)   ● or ★ depending upon filling

Cut-out pastry shapes

From trimmings of pastry cut various shapes using canapé
cutters. Brush the pastry with water to attach the shapes.
(sweet and savoury pies)   ● or ★ depending upon filling

Pastry fleurons

1 Cut a strip of flaky or puff pastry 5 cm/2 inches wide. Using a 4 cm/1½ inch diameter fluted cutter start at the base of the strip of pastry and remove crescent shapes.

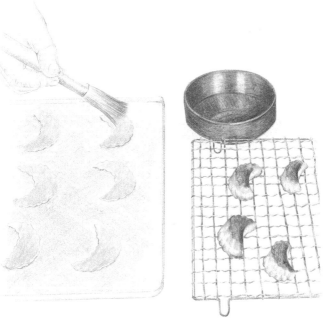

2 Brush with beaten egg and bake in a preheated hot oven (220°C, 425°F, Gas Mark 7) for about 10 minutes.
(arrange around vegetable and fish dishes or casseroles)
● or ★ depending upon filling, or keep separate in sealed container

Lattice work

Cover the top of an open tart or flan with 5 mm - 1 cm/¼ - ½ inch strips of pastry allowing 5 mm/¼ inch between each.

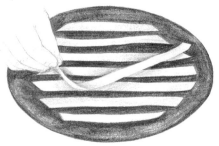

1 For plain lattice, start in the centre and place a strip of pastry at an angle across the top.

2 Leaving 5 mm/¼ inch between each strip continue from the centre to each edge. Neaten off the edges with a knife.

1 For woven lattice, place a strip of pastry across the centre at right-angles to the first layer.

2 Carefully fold back alternate strips from the first layer.

3 Lay another strip of pastry at right-angles on the tart and carefully replace the folded strips.

4 Continue folding back alternate strips of pastry and weaving strips across until one side is complete. Turn the dish round, remove the first strip across the centre and continue weaving across the other half.
(sweet or savoury flans or tarts)   ● or ★ depending upon filling

Fluted and plain tartlets

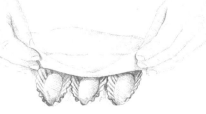

1 Arrange circular, boat-shaped or square moulds very close together and cover with a thin sheet of pastry.

2 With a small ball of dough dipped in flour carefully press the pastry into the moulds.

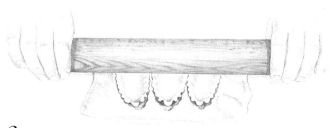

3 Roll off the excess pastry with a floured rolling pin.

4 Prick well, bake in a preheated moderately hot oven: (200°C/400°F/Gas Mark 6) for about 20 minutes for shortcrust pastry or about 15 minutes for cheese pastry; (190°C/375°F/Gas Mark 5) for about 15 minutes for sweet shortcrust pastry; then fill as required just before serving.
(fruit or savoury tartlets)   ● ★ left empty

Scalloped pastry shells

1 Butter the outside of a scallop shell and cover with a thin piece of shortcrust pastry.

2 Press the pastry firmly on to the shell and use your fingers to trim off the edge.

3 Place on a baking sheet pastry side up and bake in a preheated moderately hot oven (200°C/400°F/Gas Mark 6) for about 20 minutes.

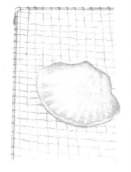

4 When cool enough to handle ease the pastry off the scallop shell with the point of a knife. Fill as required just before serving. (fish and shellfish mixtures)
● or ★ left empty

Apricot or redcurrant glaze

1 For apricot glaze, heat some apricot jam until it becomes liquid then pass it through a wire sieve into a clean pan.

2 Reheat the jam and if very thick add a little lemon juice.

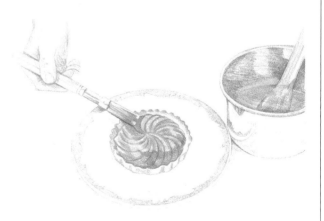

3 Brush thickly and evenly over the pastry, or spoon over a fruit filling.

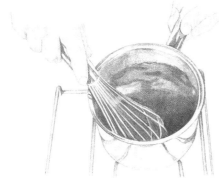

1 For redcurrant glaze, heat some redcurrant jelly and bring to boiling point, beating with a sauce whisk to remove any lumps.

2 Allow to cool slightly and then brush over the pastry or spoon over a fruit filling.
(open fruit flans, fruit tarts, lattice flans)

Piping cream

1 Whisk double or whipping cream until it forms stiff peaks. Put into a nylon piping bag containing a small rosette nozzle.

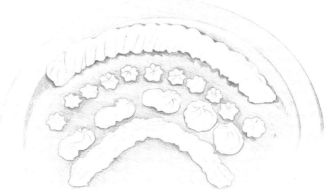

2 Hold the piping bag firmly in one hand and squeeze the bag gently to pipe your design.
(fruit flans, charlottes, cheesecakes)

Piped savoury cones

Use thin slices of ham, garlic sausage or salami to make these cones and one of the Savoury fillings (see above).

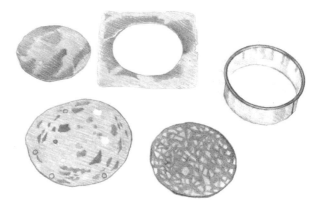

1 If using ham cut into a 7.5 cm/3 inch circle first.

2 Cut from the centre to the edge of each circle of meat. Hold each corner and twist to form a cone. To make smaller cones use half a slice of meat.

3 Using a small rosette piping nozzle, pipe any of the fillings into the cones.
(hors d'oeuvre)   □   Keep unfilled cones in refrigerator

Cocktail canapés

Using the Savoury fillings (see left) and fried Shaped croûtons (p. 45) or small Fluted or plain tartlets (p. 64) made with cheese pastry, pipe the filling on to the base and garnish as follows:

Use a halved walnut or strip of mango from chutney on the curry flavoured full fat soft cheese; half a green grape on the horseradish flavoured full fat soft cheese; a slice of gherkin on the tomato flavoured full fat soft cheese; a roasted hazelnut on the Danish blue filling; and a halved or whole cocktail onion on the liver pâté.

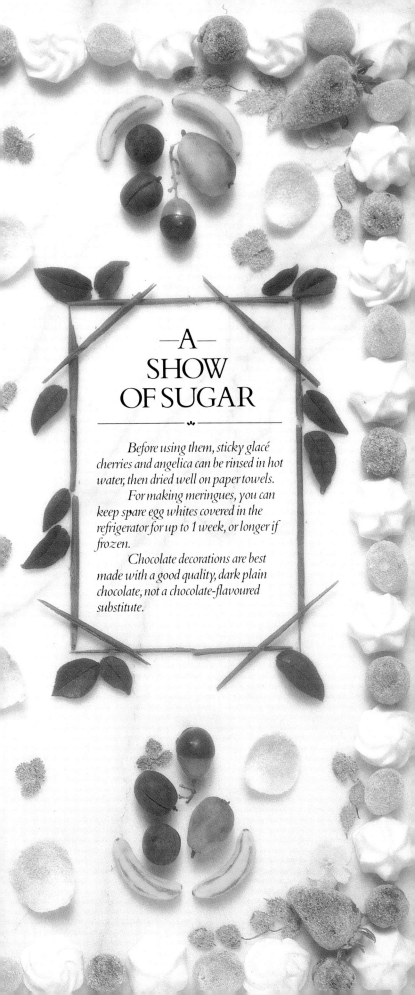

—A—
SHOW
OF SUGAR

❧

*Before using them, sticky glacé
cherries and angelica can be rinsed in hot
water, then dried well on paper towels.*

*For making meringues, you can
keep spare egg whites covered in the
refrigerator for up to 1 week, or longer if
frozen.*

*Chocolate decorations are best
made with a good quality, dark plain
chocolate, not a chocolate-flavoured
substitute.*

Petal and leaf frosting

1 Use violet, primrose and rose petals, mint, wild or small strawberry leaves and borage leaves. Gently rinse fresh undamaged petals or leaves and dry carefully with paper towels. Brush with or dip them in lightly beaten egg white.

2 Coat with a thick layer of caster sugar and dry for about 1 hour on non-stick silicone paper.
(petals and leaves for cold desserts) (leaves for drinks)

Using glacé cherries

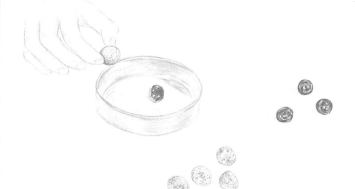

Roll whole glacé cherries in granulated sugar.

Using washed glacé cherries, cut each one into 6-8 petal shaped pieces and arrange into a flower.

Using aspic cutters cut shapes of your choice from washed glacé cherries.
(desserts, cakes)   • On or off the food

Using angelica

Cut a strip of angelica about
5 mm/¼ inch wide and make
diamond shapes.
(desserts, individual cakes)
• On or off the food

Using glacé cherries and angelica

1 Make a glacé cherry flower (see above). Cut a thin strip of angelica and use as a flower stalk.

2 Put the flower on the angelica stalk. Cut and place diamond-shaped leaves (see above) at intervals along the stalk.
(sweet tarts, individual cakes, mousses)   • On or off the food

Sugared fruits

Use strawberries, grapes, plums, damsons, or greengages.
Wash fruit and dry carefully on paper towels. Brush with lightly
beaten egg white, roll in caster sugar and leave to dry for about
15 minutes on non-stick silicone paper.
(mousses, iced desserts, after dinner fruit bowl)

Marzipan fruits

Colour a piece of
marzipan by kneading
in a few drops of appropriate liquid
food colouring.

Apple

1 Use a small piece of green
marzipan and roll it into a ball.

2 With a very fine paint
brush paint round the ball
lightly with red food
colouring. For a stalk use a
small clove.

Pear

Use a small piece of yellow/green marzipan and form into a pear shape. For a stalk use a small clove.

Banana

Make a banana shape from a small piece of yellow marzipan. With a very fine paint brush dipped in brown food colouring make lines along the banana and place a small piece of currant at the flower end.

Orange

Use a small piece of orange marzipan and roll it into a ball. Carefully roll the ball over a fine grater to mark the skin and use a small piece of clove for the flower end.

Plum

Use a small piece of deep purple marzipan and form it into an oval shape. Mark along one side with the back of a knife. When the plum is dry brush with icing sugar to give a bloom. (gâteaux, in paper sweet cases as petit fours)   ● All marzipan fruits will keep, uncovered for at least 10 days

> **MERINGUE SUISSE**
> Whisk 2 egg whites until they stand in peaks. Add 15 g/½ oz caster sugar and continue to whisk for a further 3-4 minutes. Fold in 100 g/4 oz caster sugar.

Baby meringues

Fill a nylon piping bag containing a large rosette nozzle with Meringue suisse (see above). Pipe small rosettes on to a baking sheet lined with non-stick silicone paper. Place in a very cool oven (120°C, 250°F, Gas Mark ½) for about 3 hours or until the meringues lift off the paper easily.
(desserts, petit fours, patissèrie)
● or ★ pack carefully as very fragile

> **MERINGUE CUITE**
> Sieve 250 g/9 oz icing sugar into a large heatproof bowl and add 4 egg whites. Stand the bowl over a pan of boiling water and whisk until the mixture is very thick. Meringue cuite is used for some of the decorations because it is easier to handle and holds its shape better than Meringue suisse.

Meringue hearts

Draw heart shapes on the back of a piece of non-stick silicone paper. Fill a nylon piping bag containing a large plain nozzle with Meringue cuite (see above). Line a baking sheet with the paper and pipe over the traced shapes. Place in a cool oven (140°C, 275°F, Gas Mark 1) for about 1½ hours, or until the meringues lift off the paper easily.
(arrange on or around gâteaux or desserts)   ● or ★ pack and store carefully as very fragile

Meringue nests

Fill a nylon piping bag containing a large plain or rosette nozzle with Meringue cuite (see left). Line a baking sheet with non-stick silicone paper. Pipe a ring starting in the centre and work outwards to about 6 cm/2½ inches in diameter. Continue piping on top of the outer ring. Cook as for the Meringue hearts (see left), but allow 2½-3 hours. Fill with fresh fruit and cream. (desserts, patissèrie) ● or ★ pack unfilled nests and store carefully as very fragile

Meringue butterflies

Draw butterfly shapes on to the back of non-stick silicone paper. Fill a nylon piping bag containing a small plain nozzle with Meringue cuite (see left). Line a baking sheet with the paper and pipe over the outline of each shape. Fill the body area completely with the meringue and pipe filigree in the wings. Cook as for the Meringue hearts (see left). (arrange on or around gâteaux or desserts) ● or ★ pack and store carefully as very fragile

Meringue mushrooms

1 Fill a nylon piping bag containing a large plain nozzle with Meringue cuite (p. 78). Pipe small rounds for the mushroom caps and short pointed lengths for the stalks on to a baking sheet lined with non-stick silicone paper. Cook as for the Meringue hearts (p. 78), but for about 1 hour only.

2 Make a small hole underneath the mushroom cap and fill with whipped cream.

3 Push the stalk into the cream.

4 Dust the tops lightly with powdered drinking chocolate.
(arrange on or around a chocolate log or gâteaux)
● or ★ pack and store carefully as very fragile

Meringue swans

1 Fill a nylon piping bag containing a large plain nozzle with Meringue cuite (p. 78). Pipe 2 pear shapes for each swan on to a baking sheet lined with non-stick silicone paper.

2 Pipe a long 'S' shape for the head and neck. Cook as for the Meringue hearts (p. 78).

3 Attach the head and neck to one of the pear shapes with whipped cream, using a small rosette nozzle.

4 Cut the other pear shape in half and place on each side to form the wings. The back of the swan can be decorated with rosettes of cream, or left plain.
(arrange on or around gâteaux or desserts) ● or ★ pack and store carefully as very fragile.

SUGAR SYRUP
Heat 450 g/1 lb sugar with 150 ml/½ pint water and stir until dissolved. Boil quickly without stirring until the mixture reaches the hard crack stage on a sugar thermometer (151°/304°F).

Dipped fruits in sugar syrup

1 Use strawberries, grapes, cherries, segments of mandarin or kumquats. With 2 lightly oiled forks or skewers dip the fruit into Sugar syrup (see above) then place on an oiled baking sheet to set.
DO NOT TOUCH WITH YOUR FINGERS.

2 When cool put in paper sweet cases.
(petit fours)

CARAMEL

Heat 225g/8 oz sugar with 65 ml/2½ fl oz water and stir until dissolved. Boil quickly without stirring until the mixture reaches the caramel stage on a sugar thermometer (185-195°C/380-390°F).

Crushed caramel

1 Pour Caramel (see above) on to an oiled baking sheet and leave to cool. When cold, crush in a food processor or in a plastic bowl with the end of a rolling pin.
(sprinkle on desserts, cakes, gâteaux) □ Keep in sealed container

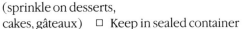

Dipped nuts in caramel

Use almonds, brazils, hazelnuts or walnuts. With 2 lightly oiled forks or skewers dip whole nuts into Caramel (see above) and place on a lightly oiled baking sheet to set.
(petit fours, gâteaux, desserts)

PRALINE

Rinse 100 g/4 oz of unblanced almonds in cold water and allow to drain. Heat 100 g/4 oz sugar with 4 tablespoons of water in a small pan and stir until dissolved. Add the almonds and boil quickly without stirring until the mixture reaches a rich brown colour and the nuts start popping (185-195°C/380-390°F on a sugar thermometer).

Crushed praline

Pour Praline (see above) on to an oiled baking sheet and leave to cool. Crush as for Crushed caramel (see left). (desserts, cakes, gâteaux) □ Keep in sealed container

GLACÉ ICING

Sieve 350 g/12 oz icing sugar into a bowl. Add about 3 tablespoons of water and beat well until smooth and shiny. Adjust the consistency with water or icing sugar as necessary.

GREASEPROOF PAPER ICING BAG

1 Cut a triangle of greaseproof paper about 28 cm/11 inches across the base and 18 cm/7 inches along the sides. Holding the base in one hand, twist the right-hand corner to the point at the top and secure with your thumb.

2 Take the left-hand corner and wrap it round to meet the point at the back.

3 Adjust the 3 points until the piping end is completely closed and sharp.

4 Fold the 3 points together to secure the bag. Cut off the piping end to use as necessary.

Feather icing

1 Coat cake with Glacé icing (p. 85). Whilst the icing is still wet fill a Greaseproof paper icing bag (p. 85) with Glacé icing in a contrasting colour. Pipe straight lines about 2.5 cm/1 inch apart across the top of the cake.

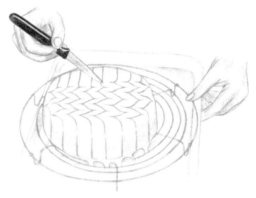

2 Quickly draw the point of a knife through the icing, first in one direction and then in the other.
• Uncovered

Spider web design

Coat a cake as for Feather icing (see above). Pipe the contrasting glacé icing in circles on the top of the cake. Draw the point of a knife through the icing from the centre to the outside edge, and in the other direction giving a spider web design.
• Uncovered

Feathering with redcurrant jelly on cream

Cover a dessert with whipped cream. Fill a Greaseproof paper icing bag (p. 85) with melted redcurrant jelly and pipe straight lines about 2.5 cm/1 inch apart across the top of the dessert. Quickly draw the point of a knife through the redcurrant jelly; either in one direction only, or first one way and then the other.

(desserts set with gelatine)   ☐ Uncovered

Below: Bavarois dessert masked with cream; decorated with redcurrant jelly feathering (above), piped cream (p. 69) and chocolate cones (p. 91) dotted with redcurrant jelly

Chocolate curls

1 Use a block of
chocolate and scrape off
curls using a potato
peeler.
(desserts, gâteaux,
cakes) ● Uncovered in
cool place

MELTED CHOCOLATE
To melt chocolate, break it into segments and melt in a heatproof
basin over a pan of hot water, without letting the basin touch the water
or allowing the steam to get into the chocolate.

Chocolate caraque

1 Spread Melted chocolate (see above) on to a rimless
baking sheet or marble slab.

2 When set, curl it off with a sharp knife, handling as little as
posible.
(desserts, gâteaux, cakes) ● Uncovered in a cool place

Coated chocolate leaves

1 Use undamaged rose or
bay leaves. Gently rinse and
dry with paper towels. Brush
the back of the leaf with a
thin layer of Melted
chocolate (see above). Allow
to set and then apply a
second coat.

2 When completely set carefully peel of the leaf.
(desserts, gâteaux)
• Uncovered in a cool place

Chocolate dipped nuts

1 Use almonds, brazils, hazelnuts or walnuts. With a fork dip the whole, skinless nuts into Melted chocolate (see left) and place on non-stick silicone paper to dry.
(serve in paper sweet cases, on gâteaux)   • Uncovered in a cool place

Chocolate dipped fruits

1 Use strawberries, grapes, cherries, small plums or segments of mandarin. Hold the fruit firmly and dip into Melted chocolate (see left) to cover half the fruit. Allow to dry on non-stick silicone paper.
(petit fours, desserts, gâteaux)

Plain chocolate cups

1 Coat the outside of a
plain tartlet tin with Melted
chocolate (p. 88). Allow to
set, then coat again.

2 Carefully loosen the
chocolate cup and lift it off
the tin.
(fill with fruit and
cream) ● Keep empty
cups uncovered in a cool
place

Fluted chocolate cups

1 Pour Melted chocolate
(p. 88) into 2 thicknesses of
fluted paper cake cases. Smooth
round with the back of a
teaspoon and when set coat the
sides again.

2 When completely set
carefully remove the paper
case.
(fill with fruit and
cream) ● Keep empty
cups uncovered in a cool
place

Chocolate medallions

Draw circles on the back of non-stick silicone paper and using a teaspoon fill the circles on the right side with Melted chocolate (p. 88). When set carefully lift the circles off the paper.
(desserts, gâteaux) ● Uncovered in a cool place

Chocolate cones

You will need to use a new icing bag for each cone so make several half size bags before you start.

1 Line a Greaseproof paper icing bag (p. 85), made from half the size of paper with Melted chocolate (p. 88) and when set apply a second coat.

2 When completely set carefully peel off the greaseproof paper. (fill with cream to decorate desserts, gâteaux)
● Uncovered in a cool place

TUILE MIXTURE

Melt 50 g/2 oz butter and allow to cool. Whisk 2 egg whites to a stiff frothy consistency. Add 65 g/2½ oz caster sugar to the whites and whisk again for 3-4 minutes until in shiny peaks. Add 50 g/2 oz sifted plain flour and fold in, together with the melted butter. Add 50 g/2 oz finely chopped blanched almonds and ½ teaspoon bought vanilla sugar. Mix carefully. Makes about 12.

Tuile cups

1 To be able to shape these cups before they harden it is necessary to work in small batches. Spread 3 teaspoons of the Tuile mixture (see above) into very thin rounds on a lightly greased baking sheet. Dust with sieved icing sugar and cook in a preheated moderately hot oven (200°C/400°F/Gas Mark 6) for about 5 minutes or until pale golden.

2 Remove from the oven, loosen immediately with a palette knife and curve round 3 lightly oiled oranges to form cups.

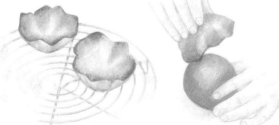

3 Allow to harden and carefully lift off. While these cups cool bake the remaining mixture in batches and form into cups. (fill with ice cream or sorbet) ● or ★ Pack empty cups carefully in a sealed container

SPONGE FINGERS

Cream 3 egg yolks with 75 g/3 oz caster sugar until light in colour and very thick. Whisk 3 egg whites until stiff and fold into the egg yolk mixture, alternately with 90 g/3½ oz plain flour sifted with 1 teaspoon bought vanilla sugar. Fill a nylon piping bag containing a large plain nozzle with the mixture. Pipe out 10 cm/4 inch lengths on to strips of non-stick silicone paper. Dust with icing sugar, tap off the surplus and cook in a pre-heated moderate oven (180°C/350°F/Gas Mark 4) for 10-13 minutes, or until the sponge fingers are pale golden in colour and firm to touch. Peel off the paper immediately and allow the sponge fingers to cool on a wire rack. Makes about 12.

● or ★ Keep in sealed container

Charlotte mould

1 Prepare the Sponge fingers (see above). Place a circle of non-stick silicone paper in the base of a charlotte mould. Cut a few of the Sponge fingers in half and trim to line the base of the charlotte mould with the sugared side downwards.

2 Using a 4 cm/1½ inch cutter remove the untidy ends from the centre of the mould and replace with a neat circle of Sponge finger.

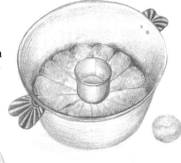

3 Trim the remaining Sponge fingers at one end and use to line the sides of the mould, with the sugared side against the mould and fitting the biscuits tightly. Use a tiny dab of butter on every second or third finger to help them stick.

4 Fill the mould as required, allow to chill and when set trim the Sponge fingers to the level of the filling. Turn out to serve. (jellies, bavarois fillings such as for Charlotte russe, mousses)
● or ★ depending upon filling

Below: Charlotte mould (left) made with sponge fingers (left) and decorated with piped cream (p. 69), frosted strawberries and strawberry leaves (p. 74)

INDEX